CONTENTS

KV-620-907

Words that look like <u>this</u> can be found in the glossary on page 24.

WHAT CAN YOU SEE?

Take a peek out of the window. What can you see? Are the trees blowing around or are they covered in something powdery and white?

WHAT'S THE WEATHER?

IT'S
SUNNY!

Written by
William Anthony

BookLife
PUBLISHING

©2021
BookLife Publishing Ltd.
King's Lynn
Norfolk PE30 4LS

All rights reserved.
Printed in Malaysia.

A catalogue record for this
book is available from the
British Library.

ISBN: 978-1-83927-194-6

Written by:
William Anthony

Edited by:
Shalini Vallepur

Designed by:
Danielle Webster-Jones

PHOTO CREDITS

All images are courtesy of Shutterstock.com, unless otherwise specified. With thanks to Getty Images, Thinkstock Photo and iStockphoto. Front Cover – MarKord, Subbotina Anna, Big Foot Productions, maxim ibragimov, SunKids. Character throughout – yusufdemirci. 4 – Fancy Tapis, Dark Moon Pictures, Iryna Alex, Tiina Tuomaala. 5 – Kichigin. 6 – Incomible. 7 – Africa Studio 8 – Africa Studio. 9 – AlinaMD. 10 – Amanda Carden. 11 – imtmphoto. 12 – wavebreakmedia. 13 – yusufdemirci, Elena Efimova. 14 – Sergey Novikov. 15 – BIGANDT.COM. 16 – werber photography. 17 – Sunny studio. 18 – DRidgway. 19 – anetapics. 20–21 – Bumble Dee. 22 – wk1003mike. 23 – Luca Santilli.

Weather is what you can see in the sky and feel in the air outside. There are lots of types of weather, such as sunshine, snow, wind and rain.

Hi! I'm the Sun, but you can call me Ray. It's nice to meet you!

SEASONS

Spring

Winter

Summer

Autumn

In many countries, there are four seasons in every year. They are spring, summer, autumn and winter. Different types of weather may happen in each season.

Summer is the warmest season. In summer, you may see lots of sunshine, but you probably won't see any snow.

Summer is when Ray comes out to play!

IT'S SUNNY!

We say it is sunny when we can see the Sun in the sky and nothing is blocking it out. The world around you will look bright and colourful.

When it's sunny, you may not see many clouds in the sky. The sky may be bright and blue.

When the weather is cloudy, I'm still shining. You just can't see me!

THE SUN

The Sun

Earth and seven other planets all move around the Sun in space.

We get sunshine from the Sun. The Sun is a big ball of burning gas. It is a very long way from Earth.

We get all of our <u>natural</u> light from the Sun. This helps us to see during the daytime. The Sun also gives us heat, which helps to keep us warm.

Happy to help!

WHAT TO WEAR

During the summer, sunny days may get quite warm. It's good to wear loose-fitting clothes such as t-shirts, skirts and shorts. These will help you to keep cool.

T-shirt

Shorts

In winter, sunny days can be cold. Don't forget to wrap up!

If you are out in the sunshine for a long time, it is a good idea to wear a hat and sunglasses. These will <u>protect</u> your head and your eyes.

Hat

Never look straight at the Sun, even with sunglasses on.

Sunglasses

FUN IN THE SUN

Sunny weather is perfect for having fun outside. Many people travel to the beach for a fun day out in the sunshine.

Have you ever built a sandcastle at the beach?

When it's hot and sunny, you could take part in water sports to cool off. You could play <u>water polo</u> or have a swimming race.

Water polo

PLANTS

Plants are living things. They need a few things to keep them alive, such as sunshine and warmth. Sunlight helps plants make the food they need in order to grow.

In spring and summer, there are lots of long sunny days. In those seasons, you can see lots of flowers and trees starting to <u>blossom</u>.

17

ANIMALS

Lots of animals <u>depend</u> on plants for food. Lots of sunshine helps plants to grow. This means there will be more food for animals to eat.

This bear is eating berries.

Some animals are <u>adapted</u> to live in sunny weather. Meerkats have dark patches around their eyes that act like sunglasses.

Looking good, meerkats!

WILDFIRES

Sometimes, the Sun can cause lots of <u>damage</u>. When an area such as a forest becomes very dry, a hot, sunny day might start a fire. This is called a wildfire.

Wildfire

Wildfires can be put out by planes, just like this plane is doing.

Wildfires can destroy lots of animal <u>habitats</u>. This means that many animals can lose their homes in a wildfire. Some wildfires can take a long time to be put out.

SAFE IN THE SUN

When you are out in the sunshine, it is important to protect yourself. Staying in the sunshine for too long can cause your skin to burn.

Ouch! Sunburn looks painful!

Sun cream will help to stop your skin from burning. A hat will keep your face in the shade. Sunglasses will protect your eyes from the bright light.

Hat

Sunglasses

Sun cream

It's also important to drink lots of water when I'm around!

GLOSSARY

adapted	changed over time to suit the environment
blossom	to produce flowers
damage	harm that is done to something or someone
depend	to rely upon or need something
gas	a thing that is like air, which spreads out to fill any space available
habitats	the natural homes in which animals, plants and other living things live
natural	found in nature and not made by people
planets	large, round objects in space (such as Earth) that travel around a star (such as the Sun)
protect	stop something from coming to harm
water polo	a game played in water by two teams who try to score by throwing a ball into a goal

INDEX